For my wonderful students, who put up with a quirky and odd teacher for so many years.

INTRODUCTION

In all my years in Japan, Hokkaido's natural wonders have held my attention the longest. Filled with geological features that I have rarely seen elsewhere, Hokkaido is a place that I could return to over and over, and it would never get old or repetitive. In this first book of my new tiny photo tour series, I will be taking you on a visual tour of one of Hokkaido's most striking locations: Jigokudani, or Hell Valley.

Why Jigokudani? It has unique volcanic features concentrated into a relatively small area. Even those with limited hiking experience and endurance can comfortably hike the area, making it the ideal natural getaway. A bonus is the general lack of foreign tourists, so you are more likely to get an authentic experience, rather than the standard tourist areas you might find in the big cities.

I intend for this to be a more visual experience, as words simply cannot do Jigokudani justice. Rather than simply reading about it, I would like you to truly see it, feel it, in the way that I did, up close and personal. If you get the chance to visit Japan, Jigokudani is worth the detour and the extra day or two necessary to get the most out of your trip. Enjoy!

GETTING THERE

Getting to Jigokudani takes a bit of time and effort. Located in Hokkaido, south and slightly east of Sapporo, the park is off the beaten track for most. If you aren't comfortable driving in Japan, public transportation is a viable alternative. Generally, you are going to want to fly into Sapporo and start from there.

While not as comprehensive as on Honshu, trains in Hokkaido still provide decent access to most regions of the island. From Sapporo, you will need to take the train from JR Sapporo Station to Noboribetsu Station, which is closest to Jigokudani. Fares start from 2,160 yen and go up to 4,480 yen, depending on the speed of the train. Expect a time frame of two to three hours. From Noboribetsu, you have the option of taking a bus or a taxi.

Both the bus and the taxi are decent options for getting around, but if you are on a budget, stick with the bus. The taxi can cost more than 2,000 yen. Costing less than 400 yen for a one-way ticket, the bus is by far the more economical choice, so long as you double-check with the driver as to the destination of the bus. In more rural areas, buses are less likely to have destinations written in English, and it is easy to get on the wrong bus. If your Japanese isn't very good, simply pick up a free pamphlet at the train station and show the driver the picture. Or show a picture from this book. They will understand. The buses only leave once or twice an hour, so be sure to have something for the wait.

On the approach to Jigokudani, you will be greeted by amazingly large statues of oni, or Japanese ogres, which stand tall over the approach. These massive statues are bright red and orange, perhaps hinting at the scorching heat to come.

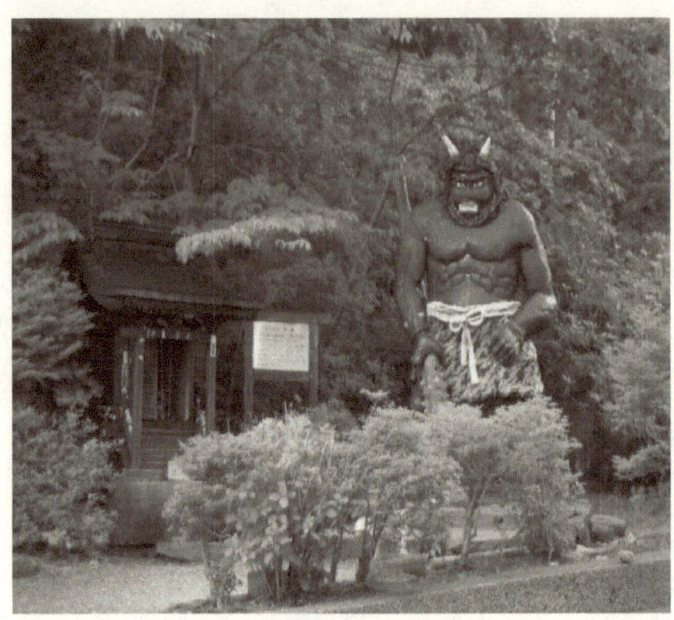

Intimidating, isn't he? An appropriate guardian at the entrance to the Noboribetsu Hot Springs Resort area. After all, no geothermal wonderland would be complete without a hot spring resort. Before the actual park lies a small area filled with hot spring hotels, shops and parks. A nice, albeit expensive place to spend an evening. As the geothermal activity isn't confined to the park itself, the tiny resort area steams and bubbles with little geysers.

Of course, this oni isn't alone. Throughout the area, smaller oni guard shrines and geysers, entrances, perhaps, to hell? This particular oni guards a small shrine. Not so scary now, is he?

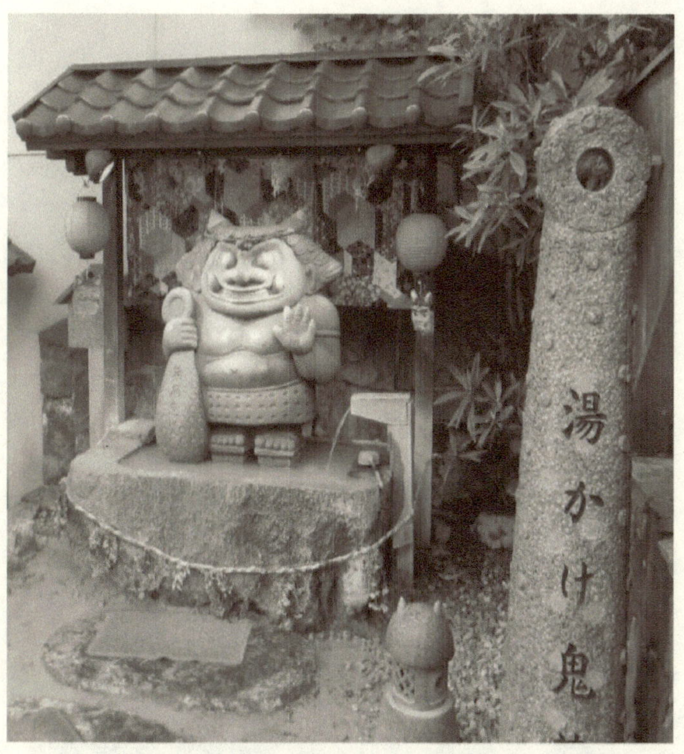

Another oni with an even bigger spiked club guards the entrance to a geyser located just off the main street. Still, given his size relative to his club, I would call him cute as well. He's ready for his bath time, with a towel and a small round cup or bucket that reads “Noboribetsu” in Hiragana.

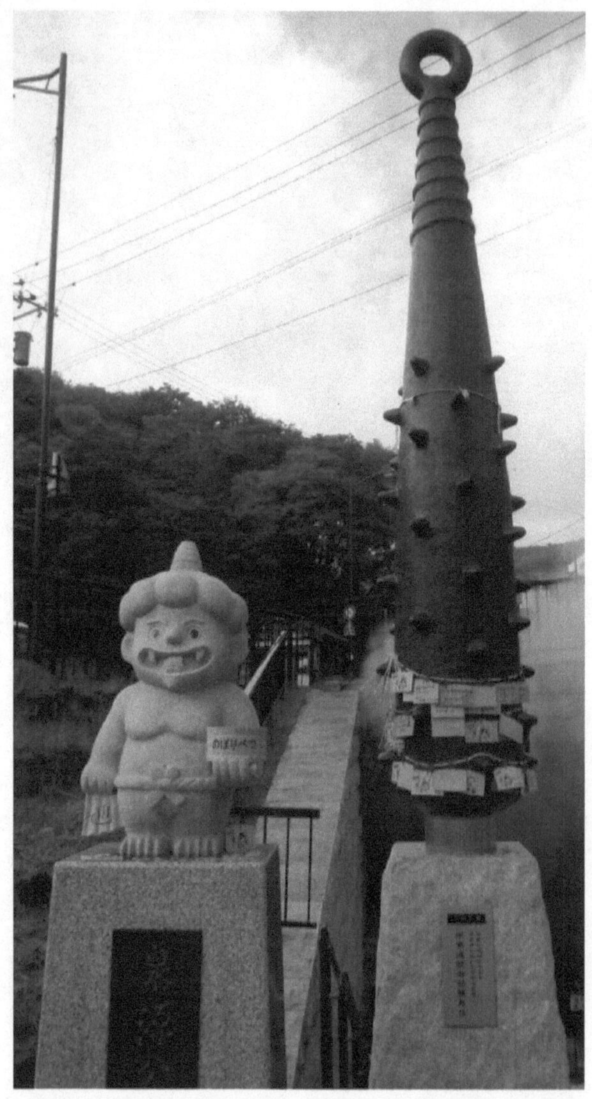

The geyser guarded by this oni is so hot that an alcove has been built around it to protect passersby. Steam constantly billows out of it, and boiling water sprays upwards regularly. Though not large or high in comparison with places like Yellowstone National Park, the close proximity is sure to impress. Tourists can walk right up near the geyser, separated by a small fence.

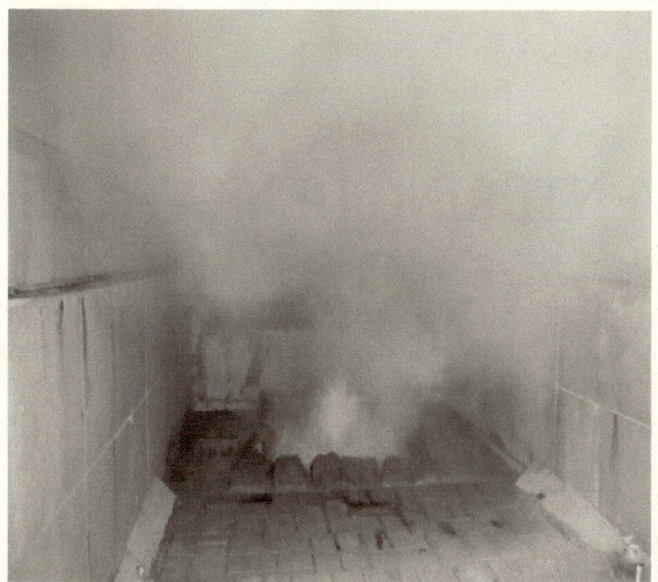

While not as impressive as a geyser left on its own out in the wild, it is still interesting in its own right, and a fun place to take selfies. Just be careful not to let your camera or phone get too wet from the steam! You are going to want to take a bath after spending time in the sulfur-scented steam.

ENTERING HELL VALLEY

Jigokudani translates to “Hell Valley,” and you will see why as soon as you enter. The sulfurous clouds that emanate from the vents throughout the valley, staining the rocks around them, the red rocks that poke out from under a thin layer of green, just around the edges...and, of course, the heat. Everything is reminiscent of a furnace, the heat just barely contained. The valley itself has a harsh kind of beauty, the kind that says, “look, don't touch.” When you enter, be warned: do not stray off the path. Off of the boardwalk, your safety is highly in doubt. Still, as the path winds through the valley, you get the opportunity to see the power of nature up close.

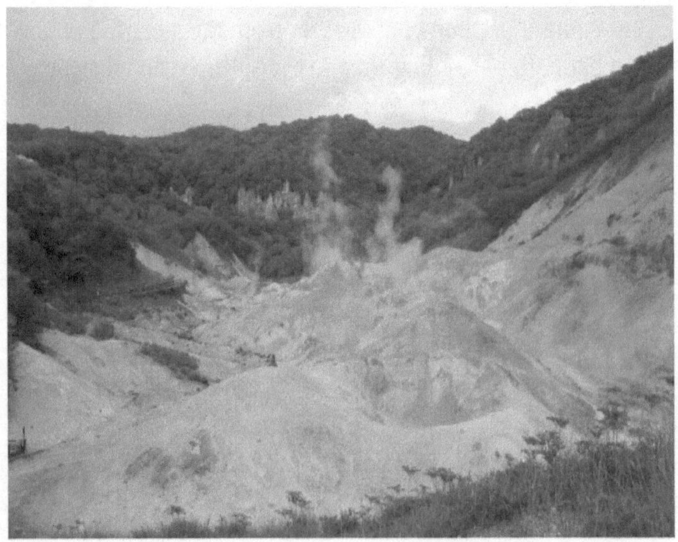

The center of the valley is full of danger. Craters and vents fill the center, and the path skirts the area, not daring to go farther in. Greenery still fights to survive along the cooler edges, but the center is far too hot.

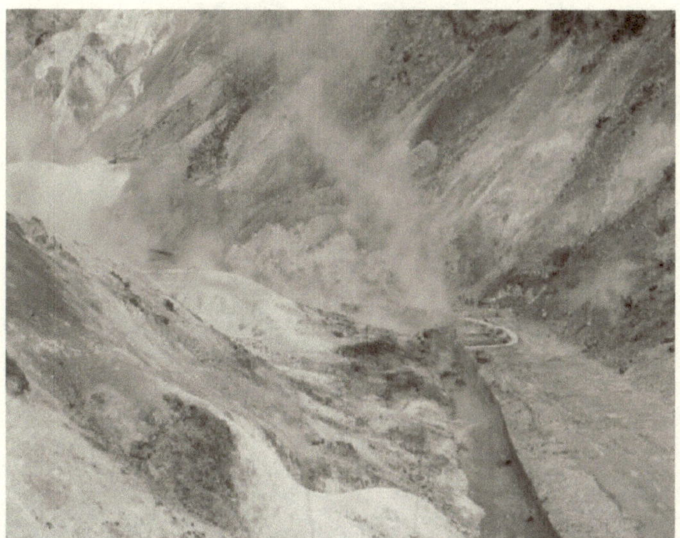

While this clear-cut channel in amongst the ridges leads into a vent, it is unclear the purpose of the machinery at the edge. The landscape is almost otherworldly in places, more reminiscent of Mars than Earth. Getting that close to a vent would be almost unbearably hot.

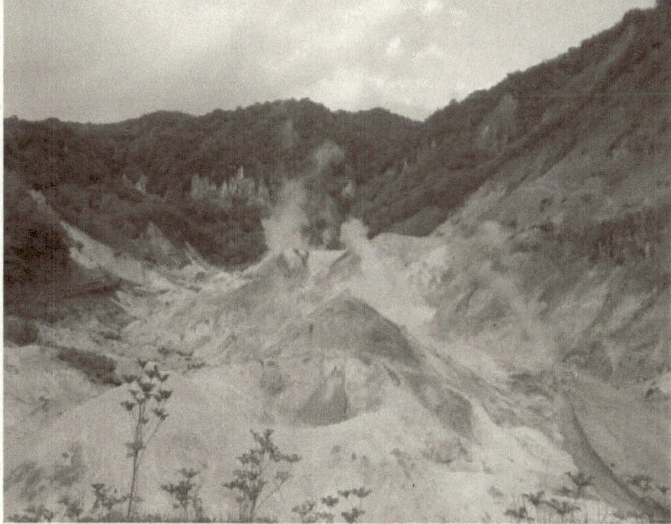

Of course, looking out over the valley, it is difficult to see any area that wouldn't be hot. As you walk through the valley, the craters are more exposed and visible, and everywhere you look, steam is seeping out of vents both large and small.

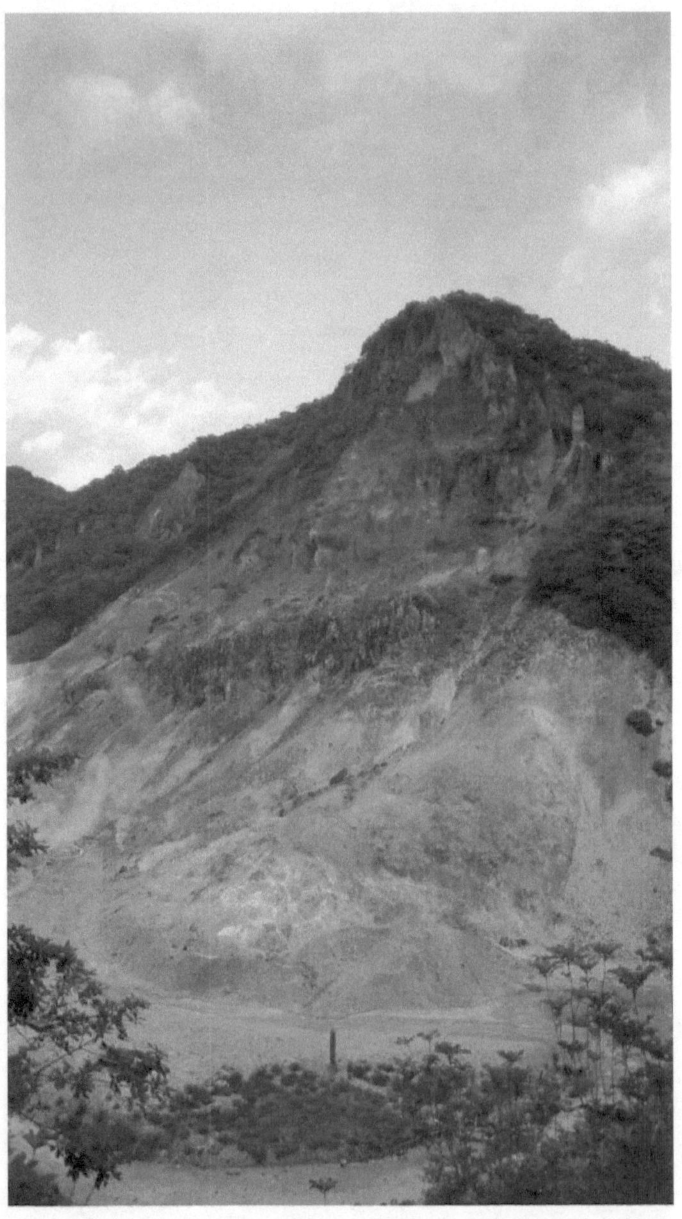

Looking up, the steep, multicolored valley walls tell a story of a long history of geological upheaval, with layers of different kinds and colors of volcanic rock exposed due to erosion. Here, the reddish-brown soil peels away to expose the gray rock underneath.

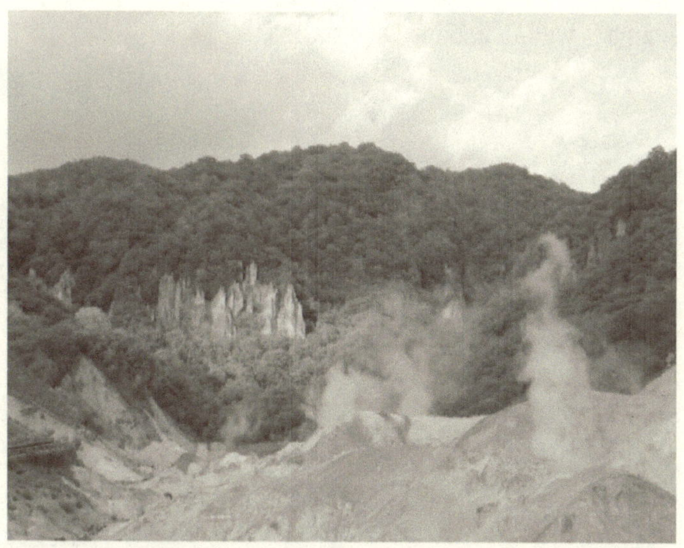

Going around the edge of the steaming vent, the smell of sulfur almost overwhelming, the trail winds its way off in the distance. Always staying to the edge of the vents, it still comes incredibly close to the action. The landscape at times seems almost alive.

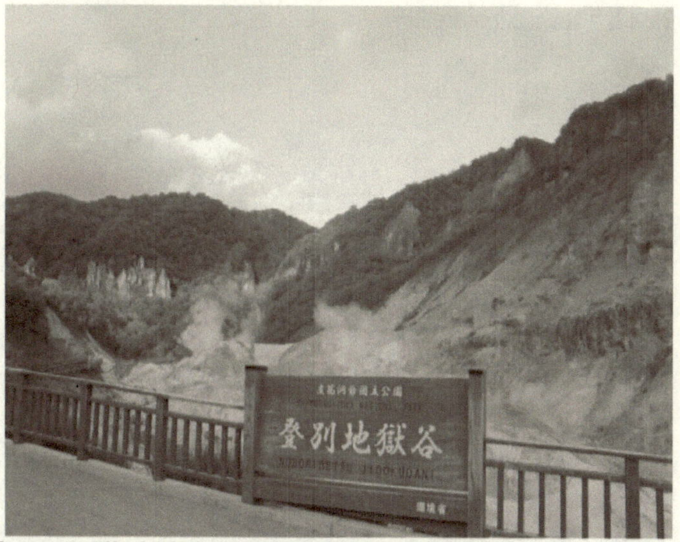

Standing proudly before a panorama of green and red, this nearly-new sign proudly proclaims this to be Shikotsu-Toya National Park, Noboribetsu Jigokudani. Shikotsu-Toya is a large national park, containing many amazing volcanoes and other natural wonders. As part of the national park, this particular area is well-maintained and staffed.

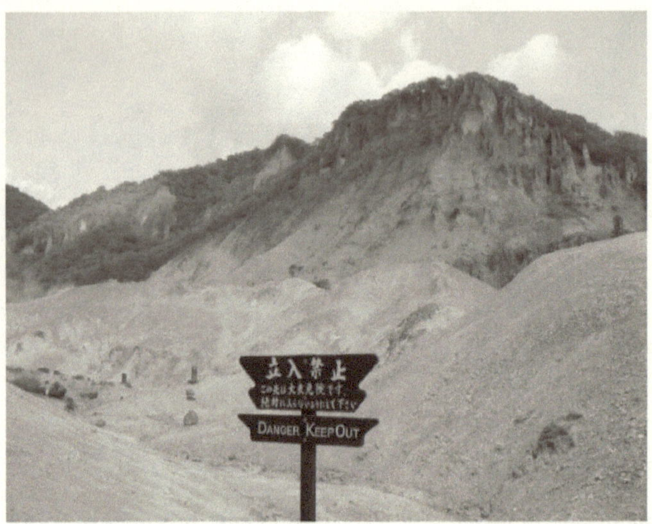

As you progress further and further into the valley, the red earth gives way to gray rock and gravel, treacherous terrain likely to crumble and send you sliding toward the vents. Thus, "Danger, Keep Out" signs were placed. Hopefully, no one will be tempted to leave the safety of the path to go exploring in the forbidden area.

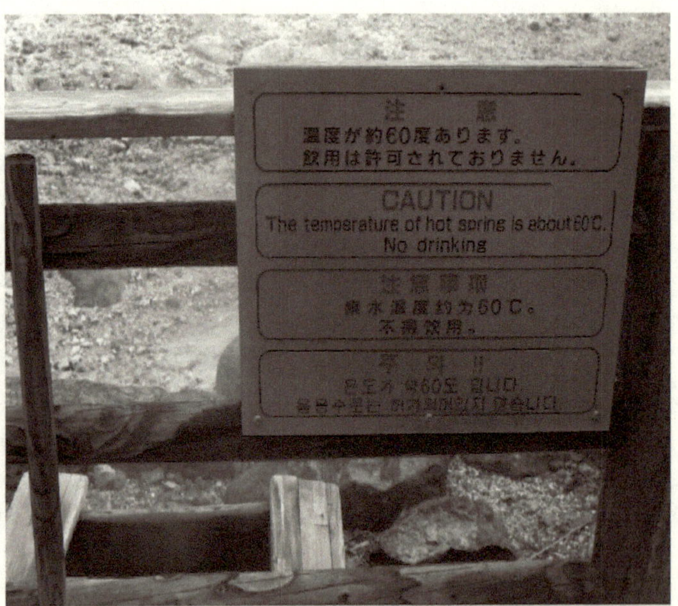

60 degrees Celsius might not sound like much, but at 140 degrees

Fahrenheit, the water coming out of the hot spring is definitely hot enough to cause severe damage. That is why it is separated from the path by a small wooden fence. Warnings are given in multiple languages, but it is ultimately up to you to keep yourself and any small children safely away from the water.

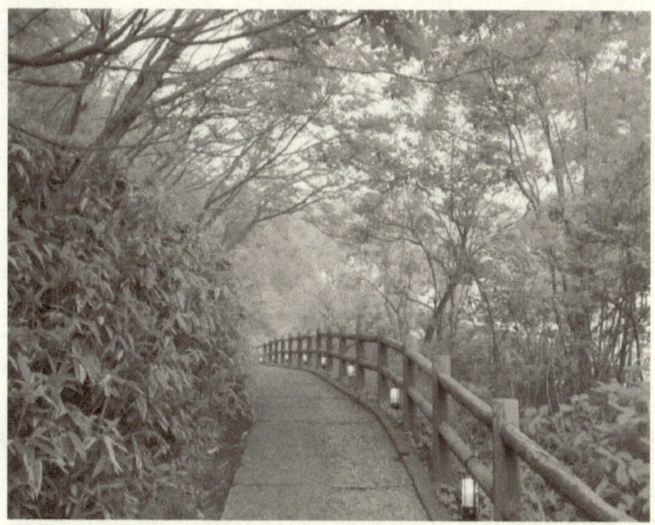

After a while, you take a short tour through the green forest. Pleasantly lit by small lanterns, the path leads you under a light canopy of trees, away from the heat of the valley.

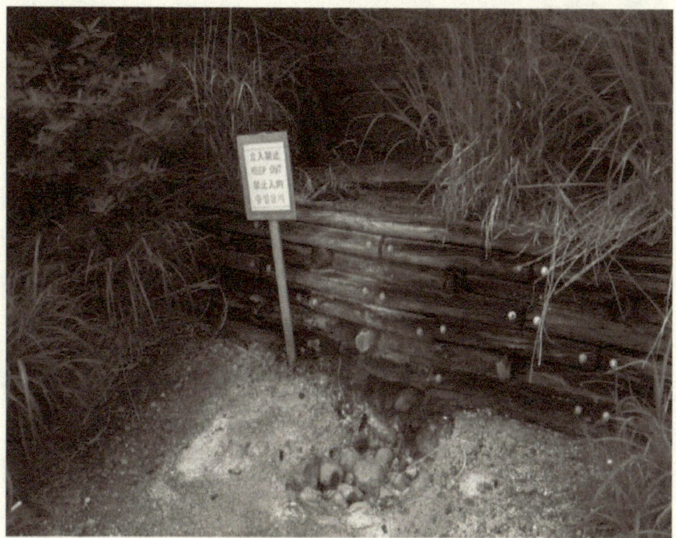

Of course, even here there are hazards to be aware of, such as this smoking vent covered by rocks. Watch where you step! Stay on the path, as you cannot see all of the tiny hidden vents in the brush.

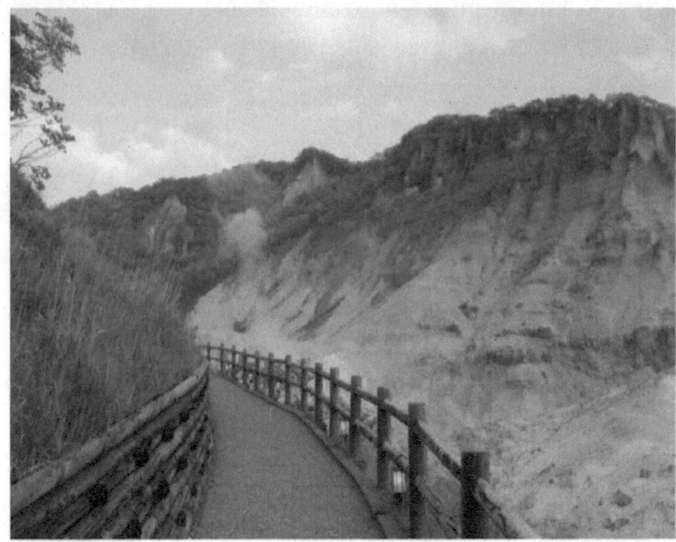

Emerging from the trees, you once again come out to the edge of the large vent, more steam rising in the distance. The trail winds around through the area, with little branches leading off to different unique features.

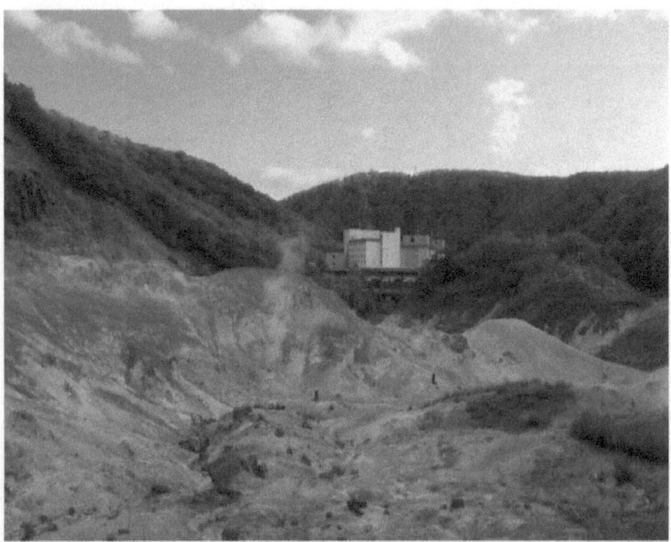

Looking back through the valley, you can see the hot spring resorts in the distance. The view would be well worth the smell of sulfur that permeates the valley.

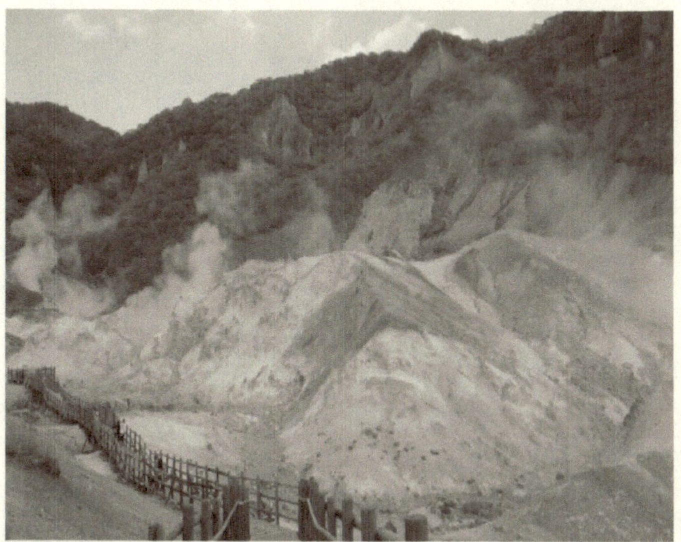

Rounding the curve, a large steaming ridge of rock comes into view, edged with a stream of boiling gray water. The path curves off to the left, twisting and turning. Far in the distance, it edges closer and closer to the vents.

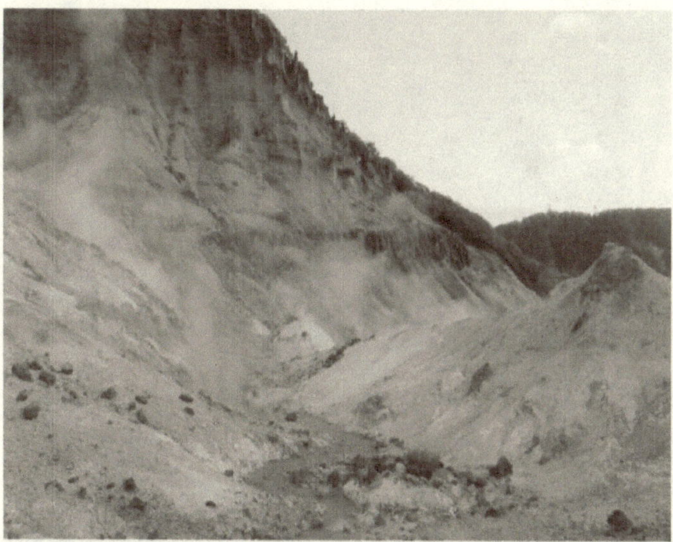

Further down the path, you get a clearer view of the river as it flows through the valley, dark gray and certainly not safe to touch. Steam rises from the vents along its path.

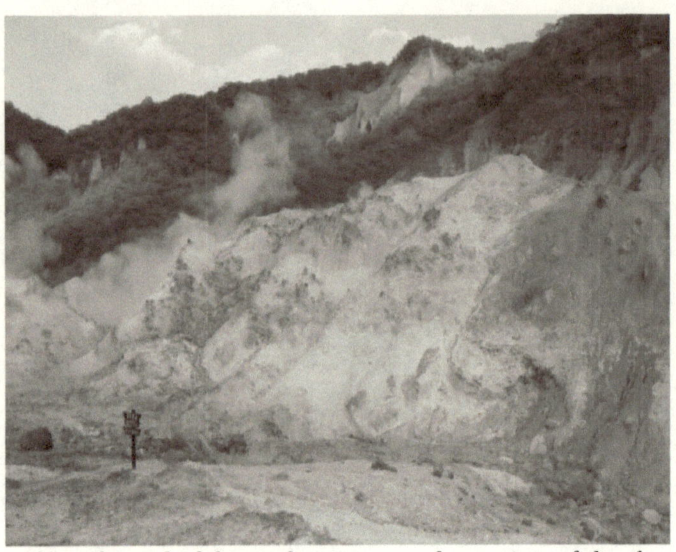

Approaching the end of this path, you get a closer view of the slopes on the edge of the valley. On a sunny day, the contrasting red, blue, orange, green and white make for a spectacular sight. Along the edge, a sign warns of the danger the area poses.

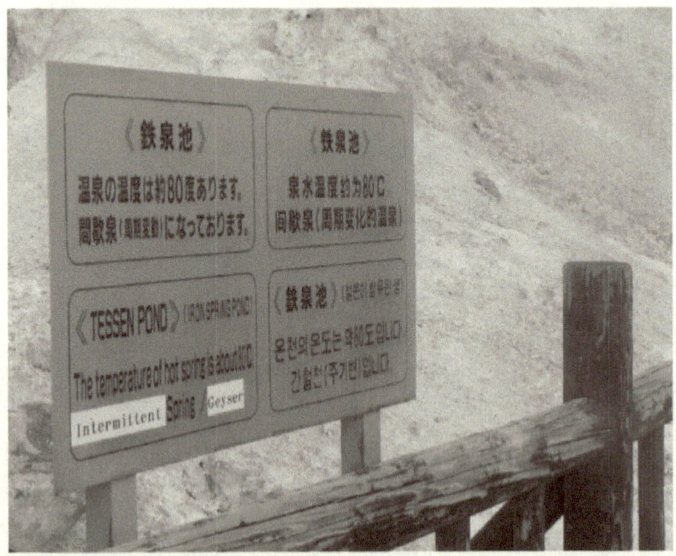

At the end of the path, there is a warning sign. This particular pond is called "Tessen Pond" or "Iron Spring Pond," and is 80 degrees Celsius or 176 degrees Fahrenheit. It is also an intermittent geyser with no regular intervals noted, so take care to keep away from it, and make sure to keep a close watch on small children if you bring your kids.

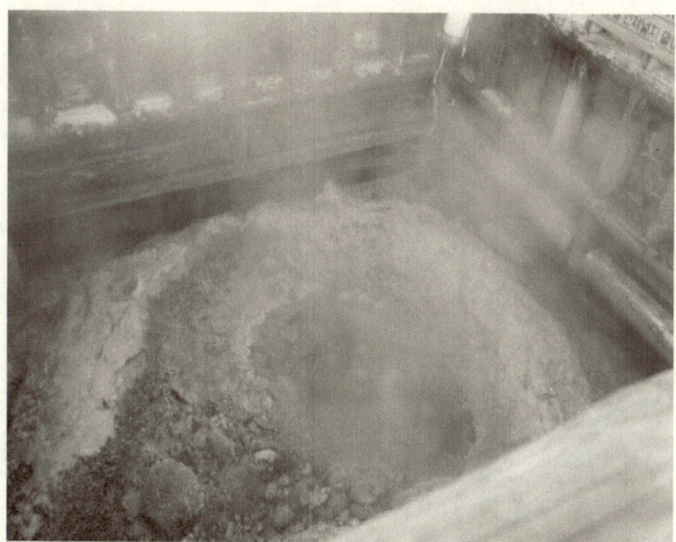

This geyser is up close. In order to give visitors a good close look, this particular geyser is set into the path. Located at the end of this path, the walkway forms a square around the geyser, allowing visitors within a few feet of it. While relatively small, it is still impressive in its own way.

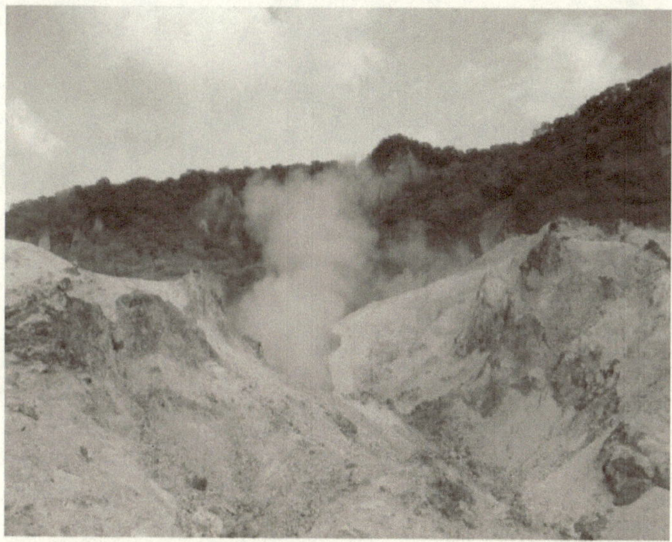

The view beyond the end of the trail. More steam emanates from a large crack in the landscape.

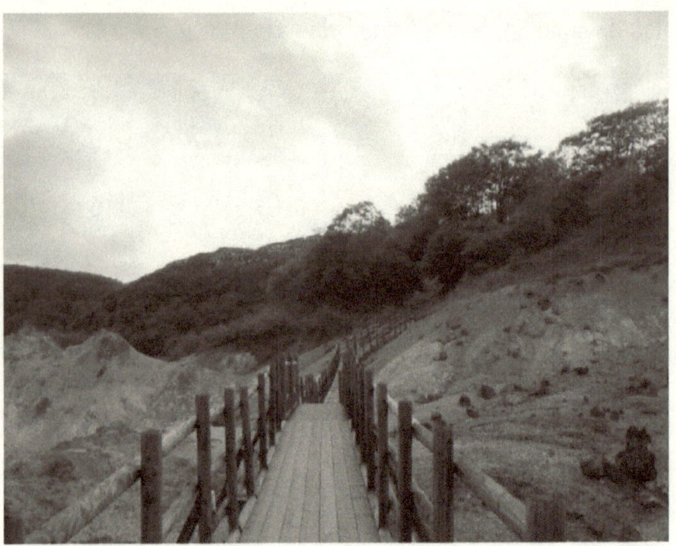

Doubling back from the end of the path, you make your way upwards until you come to a branch in the path. There, you can either continue back towards the entrance, or follow the path up the hill.

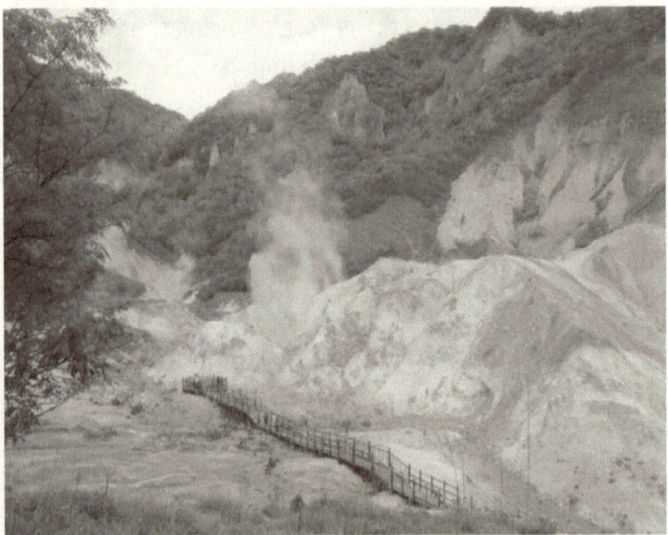

From the hillside, you can see the end of the valley spread out below. The path is the only sign of civilization among the otherwise desolate landscape.

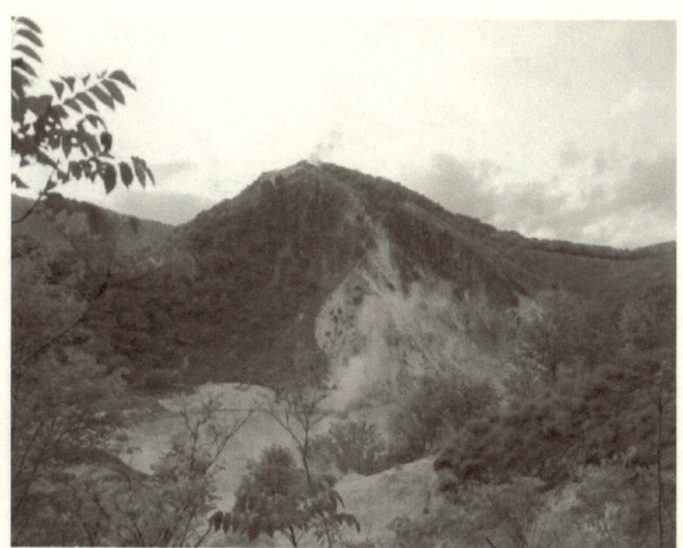

Once you get to the top of the ridge, you are greeted with the most amazing sight: a boiling lake at the base of a smoking volcano. The trees recede just enough to offer spectacular views, amazing in any season.

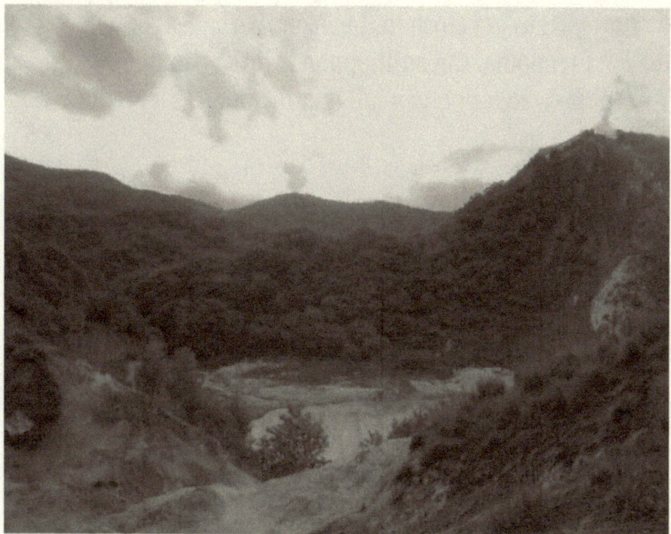

As you continue onward, the view opens up even more, offering glimpses of green mountains in the distance, and a more direct look at the lake. The scene is calm and peaceful, save for the chatter from a few fellow hikers.

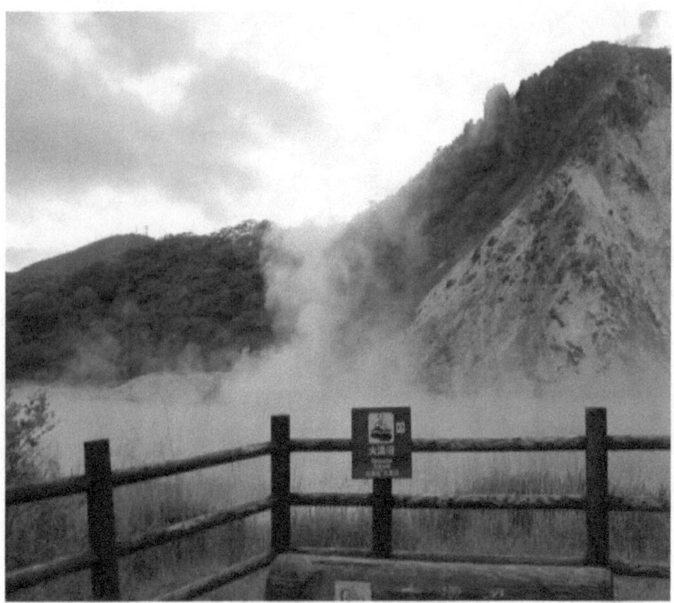

A short distance further and the trail leads you downward to the viewing area. While there is a less-than-picturesque parking lot behind, the viewing area does allow you to get close to the lake. A small sign tells you that you have arrived at Oyunuma, the boiling pond. Just by looking at the steam rising off from the water, you can tell that the pond is incredibly hot.

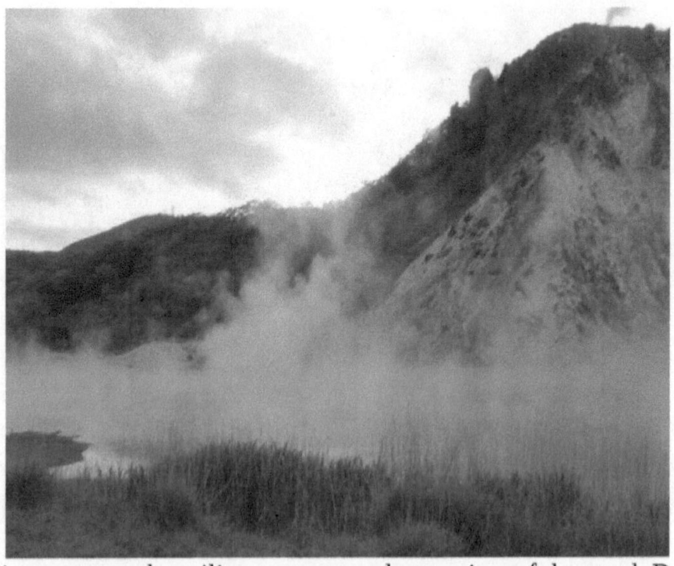

Looking out over the railing, you get a clearer view of the pond. Despite the heat, lush green grass grows nearly to the edge of the water, adding a beautiful touch of color. The water looks almost silvery, where not covered with steam.

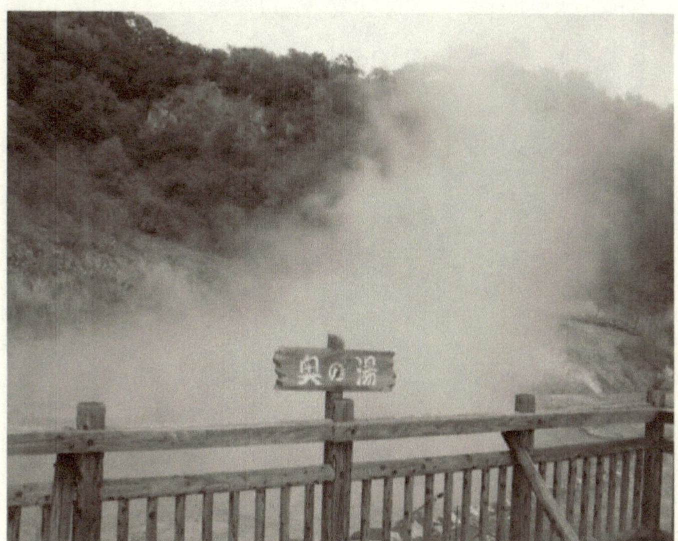

Across the parking lot from Oyunuma is a smaller, even smokier pond. The fences and signs are a lot older, but still in good shape. Clearly not the star of the area, it is still well-worth checking out. It is fairly quaint.

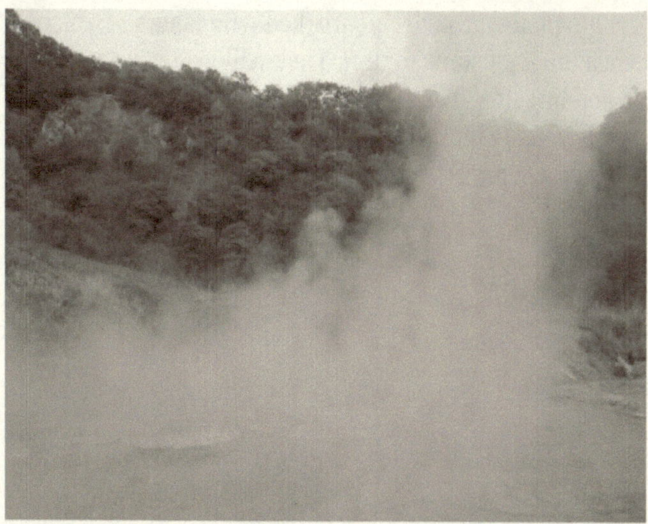

Looking down into the pond, you can see a gray and murky-looking liquid, smelling of sulfur. When taking pictures at this close of a distance, take care to clean your camera lens or cell phone frequently, as the moisture in the air can cause damage.

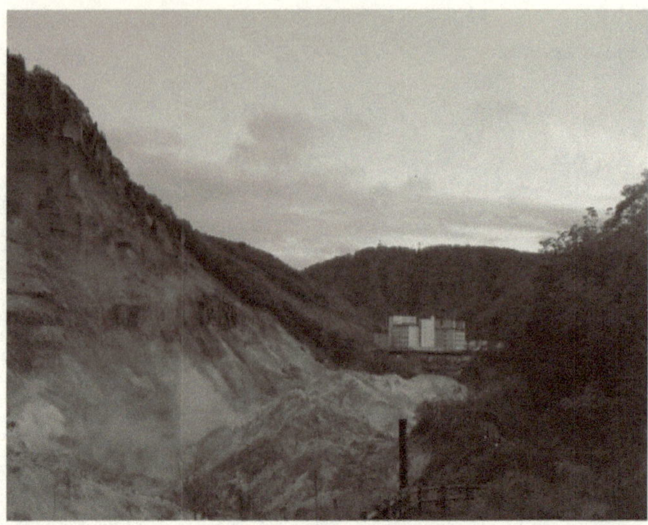

After enjoying your time at the ponds, it is time to start heading back. Along the way, if you have time, take the side trails. If you have aching feet, you can soak them in the natural hot springs. The path to a hot stream suitable for soaking away foot pain is clearly marked in English, and there is really no chance of getting lost if you stay on the paths. And if you find yourself running late, the paths are marked with lanterns, which automatically light up when the light starts to dim. They will lead you safely back to the resort area and bus stop. There, you can buy a few souvenirs, have a snack or grab dinner. If you are lucky enough to be there on the right day, you might even experience a summer festival. Enjoy!

AFTERWORD

I hope that you have enjoyed this tiny photo tour! I love going off the beaten track, and sharing these places with others who might not have heard of them. I hope that I have helped to inspire you to venture out into the lesser-known places as well! After all, Japan is far more than Tokyo and the other big cities. There is so much more to do and see, but deciding what to do when you have a limited time available can be a challenge.

I urge anyone visiting Japan: if you have the time, consider going up to Hokkaido and visiting Jigokudani. It may seem like a big challenge to get around Japan, but once there, I think that you will find it very easy and convenient. If you are thinking of traveling to multiple locations around the country, the local discount airline, Peach, can take you between most major cities for less than 10,000 yen one way. Between Osaka and Sapporo, tickets can run as low as 4,000 yen. If you are on a budget and want to maximize your time, this is definitely a viable option, and one which I have utilized on a regular basis.

If you like this book and it helped you in some way or another, kindly post a review on Amazon.com.

www.ingramcontent.com/pod-product-compliance
Lightning Source LLC
LaVergne TN
LVHW041308150826
845673LV00008B/2789